Home Time

A BOOK TO ENTERTAIN YOUR CHILD

STICKY FINGERS

Written and compiled by Judy F Taylor
Illustrated by Anne Parsons and Helen Marsden

Home Time is a series of six books, each designed to give the busy parent bright ideas!
Each chosen item has been tested with children of various ages with much success.
You will find fresh ideas, with clear instructions, to interest and entertain your child
throughout the year, in any weather, using only basic materials or ingredients.

HENDERSON
PUBLISHING PLC
©1995 HENDERSON PUBLISHING PLC

STICKY FINGERS

The activities in this book range from simple to more challenging. Most use materials you are likely to have at home. For others, the basic requirements are a sheet of art card, a sheet of sugar paper, and a stick of paper glue. Papers and card can be found at many stationers and art and craft shops. If your child enjoys creating things, it may be worth keeping a small stock of coloured papers and card available, so that their efforts can look most effective.

AUTUMN LADY

Autumn is a lovely time of year to go out for a walk, and scrunch through piles of fallen leaves. Encourage children to gather dry and different shaded leaves, to create this pretty Autumn Lady. Tell them to search for vibrant colours, scarlets, greens and gold, and find flat ones.

Suggest a game to collect as many different leaves as possible, and try naming them.

Materials:
- thick art card
- coloured pencils
- all-purpose glue
- selection of dry leaves and grasses

Method:

1 Draw the outline of a lady in a long dress. Colour in her face.

2 Sort out the largest leaves, and start gluing them to form the bottom of her long dress. Make sure they all face downwards. Continue to glue leaves to cover her skirt.

3 Pick smaller leaves and glue onto her bodice. Add two long leaves for her arms.

4 To finish, choose long grasses for her flowing hair, glue in place. If you wish, you can make a tiny leaf hat to match, or paint on a flowery headdress of gold and orange flowers.

LEAF PRINT PAPER

Again, set the children to searching for leaves, taking note of their texture and varied shapes.
They will find it easier to use larger leaves for this exercise.
Gather quite a number, as they soon become soggy when printing starts.

Materials:
- leaves
- art paper, coloured or plain
- paints
- paintbrushes
- plenty of newspaper to avoid mess

Method:

1 Lay a dry leaf on newspaper. Paint over one side.

2 Press the painted side onto the art paper. Smooth it down and apply some pressure, so that a good print is made.

3 Repeat the process, until the paper is covered with leaf prints. Suggest an effective overlapping pattern, using different paint colours.
Or a border pattern, around the edge of the paper only, with a different leaf shape printed in the centre.

4 Once children can do this neatly, they can progress to smaller items like gift tags or greetings cards.

LEAF PRINT

BARK RUBBINGS

Making rubbings is an interesting way to discover different types of trees. This works best when the barks are dry. Children can make a collection of their own and mount them in a scrap book. You may need to help them identify each bark, comparing their rubbings to pictures in an illustrated tree book from the library.

Materials:
- sheets of strong paper
- thick wax crayons
- sticky tape

Method:

1 Choose a tree with an interesting bark pattern. Tape paper to the tree.

2 Using the side of a wax crayon, start crayoning over the bark. Use the other hand to keep the paper flat against the trunk, as the paper may tear. An imprint will begin to appear.

HOLD PAPER FLAT

3 Make different bark rubbings with different shades of wax crayon.

4 Children can experiment with different papers, for the best effects.

5 Mount in a scrap book and label its name, date and location, to provide an interesting reference for your child later on.

YOU COULD ALSO STICK IN DRIED LEAVES AND LEAF PRINTS FROM THE SAME TREE

FARMYARD CREATURES

For this design, natural seeds and grasses are used to create unusual seed collage. Children could trace the shape of the chicken or cockerel from a picture, if they are unsure how to draw one. You could add to the collection by including a donkey, or some ducklings.

Materials:
- pumpkin and sunflower seeds
- gold, red and green grasses
- split peas
- acorn shells or other nut shells available
- coloured felt-tip pens
- thick card
- all-purpose glue

Method:

1 Draw or trace the outline of a chicken.

2 Using felt-tip pens, colour pumpkin seeds red, orange and brown, for the chicken's feathers.

3 Glue a split pea in position for the hen's eye. Outline it in black felt-tip pen. Stick on two melon seeds for claws on end of legs. Draw a sharp beak in red. Colour in her comb red.

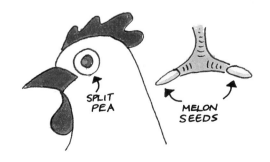

SPLIT PEA

MELON SEEDS

4 Now start building up her body with the pumpkin seeds. Spread some glue on the card first, then carefully overlap the seeds, trying to alternate the colours to resemble feathers. Carry on until the entire body is covered.

STICK ON SEEDS

5 Cut some red and orange grasses to shape her tail. Glue in place.

To add interest, the hen could be pecking at a small pile of melon seeds and nuts, glued onto the picture.

COTTON WOOL CHICK

USE REAL EGG SHELL PIECES AND GRASS OR STRAW

YOU COULD USE NATURAL COLOURED SUNFLOWER SEEDS FOR THE DONKEY

FLUFFY COTTON WOOL DUCKLINGS

MINIATURE PLATE GARDEN

All children love digging around in the garden. This design gives them their very own version. When the flower heads die, they can be replaced with fresh ones.

Materials:
- large old dinner plate, biscuit tin lid or seed tray
- clean soil
- assortment of small twigs, leaves, flower heads
- small pebbles
- egg cup
- scissors

Method:

1 Fill the plate or seed tray with soil. Dampen a little.

2 Now work out the garden plan. Will it have a hill, a wood, a pond or rockery?

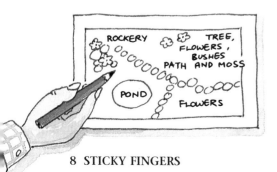

3 Cut off flower heads, small twigs and leaves for your child to put in position. A trickle of pebbles creates a winding path.

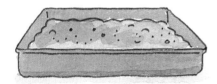

4 Sink the egg cup into the soil, filled with water, for a pool.

Of course, small figures from the toy cupboard can be added.

For an interesting idea, keep a miniature garden going all the year round, starting with Spring right through to Winter time. Change the flowers and twigs to suit the seasons.

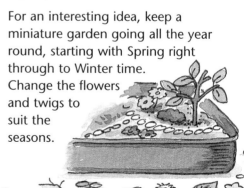

GROW YOUR AGE IN FLOWERS

Here is another natural idea to help children understand about growing things. Any flower seeds are suitable, but be sure to pick bright and colourful varieties that will bloom at roughly the same time of year, and grow to the same height.

Materials:
- clear patch of soil bed
- packets of flower seeds (annuals)
- stick
- garden tools

Method:

1 Rake over the bed before you start, to ensure a smooth surface. Children of all ages can be encouraged to help prepare their own little plot.

2 With a stick, draw out the numbers of your child's age. Keep the numbers large and the same size. Needless to say, if their birthday comes before the flowers bloom, increase the number drawn.

3 Sprinkle on the seeds, rake over a light layer of soil, and water lightly.

4 When the seeds grow, the numbers should appear in flowers.

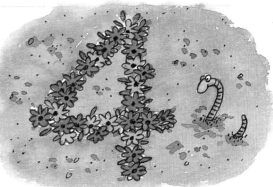

Some seeds may not germinate, so sow them fairly thickly. For the best effect, the numbers should stand in a clearing, or among shorter flowers. Children will take great pride watching the progress of 'their age' growing, and lending a hand to water during dry weeks.

HETTY AND HENRY EGGHEAD

Boys and girls alike can grasp the concept of growing seeds indoors. In fact, you can create an entire family of Eggheads, naming them after friends, pets and family.

Materials:
- clean empty egg shells (mum or dad will need to put these by after breakfast or baking)
- cotton wool
- cress seeds
- felt-tip pens
- egg cup

Method:

1 Using felt-tips, draw a funny Hetty and Henry face on the eggs.

2 Moisten cotton wool and pack into the egg.

3 Sprinkle some cress seeds on top of the cotton wool.

4 Stand in an egg cup and leave in a light place. A window ledge is ideal. Check that the cotton wool is kept moist.

In a few days, the Eggheads will grow lovely green hair. The arguments might start, however, when it's time to decide which Egghead has a haircut into the sandwiches!

FLOWERY HAT

Girls might have more fun with this than the boys, but don't rule it out if you have an old straw hat in the loft! The finished item can be worn, of course, or it makes a charming wall decoration.

As a long term project, children will thoroughly enjoy gathering and drying the ingredients to decorate their hat later.

Materials:
- any straw hat
- small dried flowers (larkspur and small rosebuds are ideal)
- light dried grasses (avoid heavy foliage, it's hard to stick on)
- all-purpose adhesive
- satin ribbon (for streamers)

Method:

1 Carefully cut off all the flower heads and think about your design before you start gluing.

2 Put a blob of glue on top of the hat, right in the centre. Stick on a little circle of flowers.

3 Fold the ribbon in half, cut both ends neatly, glue onto back of hat, just beneath the crown. Glue a couple of flowers on the top of the ribbon, and some on the brim by the ribbon.

4 Moving on to the brim of the hat, stick on a ring of flowers. Then stick on some small pieces of grass, to form an attractive pattern, placing them close to the edge of the brim.

CHRISTMAS GARLAND

The tradition of gathering green holly and fir to welcome in Christmas goes back many hundreds of years. Here is a garland based on natural ingredients to echo these themes, and bring a country feel to your family's festivities.

Materials:
- twig wreath (bought from florists, or fun to make with long hazel twigs wound around an old wire coat hanger stretched into a circle - an adult should shape and trim the wire with pliers)
- dried wheat heads
- dried grasses
- holly
- ivy
- Cypress fir
- bay leaves
- green ribbon

Method:

1 Sort out all the dried material and plan a loose design. Cut stems leaving enough to twine into wreath.

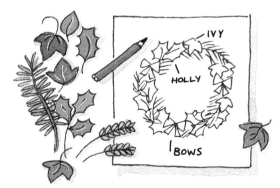

2 Begin by weaving the pieces of fir into the wreath to form a background.

3 Next, add the holly and ivy. Try and follow the same direction, so that the design flows one way.

4 Carry on adding all the pieces of material, until the wreath is covered. Add smaller details like wheat heads and bay leaves last.

5 Make ribbon bows, leaving long ties, and attach at intervals among the foliage.

RAINBOW FIR CONES

Whilst children may be looking for grasses to dry, leaves to print, or barks to rub, they can keep an eye open for fir cones. These are useful material for very simple decorations and this idea is something different.

Materials:
- quantity of small, dry fir cones
- gold or silver metallic spray paint
- glitter dust
- strips of tinsel
- scissors
- newspaper for spraying onto

Method:

1 Begin by opening the fir cones; just leave them in a warm place for a few days, or if you want to speed up the process, place in an oven, spread out on a baking tray. They will unfurl in the heat. Be careful you don't overcook them, though.

2 Spray cones gold and silver. (Small children need close direction here.) Before the spray dries, sprinkle on coloured glitter. A good tip here is to use a polythene bag to hold the glitter and drop in the cones, then none is wasted.

3 Attach the sparkling cones to a festive tree, or wall lamps perhaps, using tinsel twined around each cone.

For a more 'natural' look, simply glue along the edges of unpainted cones, and add glitter to this. Glitter-glue pens are very handy for drawing straight onto the cone-tips.

MAGIC TREE

The magic tree design can be used as an Easter or Christmas idea, just vary the decoration on the tree, and the covering on the flower pot. Make it with the help of a youngster, or simply supply these guidelines to stimulate an older child.

Materials:
- small dry branch
- clean flower pot
- soil and moss
- empty egg shells (in halves)
- coloured ribbon
- sheet of wrapping paper
- all purpose glue
- little wrapped sweets or chocolates
- paints

Method:

1 Carefully wrap the clean flower pot with pretty paper. Stick the top part over the rim of the flower pot.

2 Paint the dry branch, either white for Christmas, or green for Easter. Allow to dry.

3 Put the soil into the flower pot. Place the painted branch into the soil. Cover with moss, making sure the branch is secure.

MOSS

4 Check the eggs shells are completely clean and dry. Cut some ribbon lengths, and stick half the ribbon around the egg shells.

5 Attach the egg shells to the branch, tie with a bow. Fill the shells with small sweets or chocolates.

The Christmas version could have glittery ribbon and more bows. It makes an attractive table decoration.

JEWELLED EGGS

These make a very pretty Christmas or Easter decoration, arranged in an empty gold chocolate box, or heaped in a bowl. Hunt around for alternative materials - the sewing box or broken costume jewellery may produce glittery bits which could be used here.

Materials:
- cold, hard boiled egg
- selection of glitter dust
- sequins (optional)
- Christmas sticky tape
- all-purpose glue
- paintbrush
- egg cup

Method:

1 Check the egg is completely cold before you start decorating. Cut a length of coloured tape and position round the centre of the egg.

2 Cover one half of the egg with glue, and sprinkle on glitter dust. Place in egg cup to dry.

3 When the first half is absolutely dry, decorate the remainder of the egg.

4 Sequins (or tiny beads) can be glued on in a pattern between rows of glitter dust. If you don't want to use glitter, coloured varnish will set the 'jewels' in place.

Children will love to make a number of these, all slightly different.

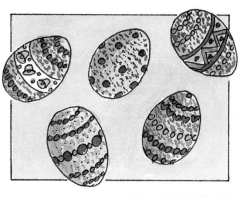

FREE-RANGE THE OWL

Egg blowing is a fairly delicate operation and therefore probably better suited for older children.

Materials:
- egg
- darning needle
- bowl
- sticky tape
- cup
- dough
- paper
- glue

Method:

1 Hold the egg under running cold water. Gently dry it.

2 Attach a piece of sticky tape to both ends of the egg. Push the needle through the tape on the widest end through to the thinner end. Wiggle the needle tip around inside the egg to break up the yolk.

3 Over a bowl, peel off both pieces of tape. Blow through the top of the egg until the contents are forced out the bottom. (Of course, you can keep the contents for later use.)

BLOW THROUGH TOP HOLE

CONTENTS OF EGG

4 Rinse the egg shell and leave to dry.

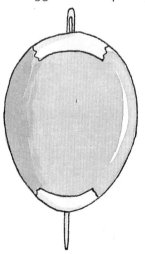

5 Place dry egg on top of an upturned cup. (Hold it in place with dough). Paint the shell light brown, adding breast feathers, white eyes and a yellow beak.

DOUGH

AND HIS FRIENDS

6 Feet can be made from painted dough. The ears are triangles of black paper and the wings come from brown paper.

Feed the child's imagination and you may find you run out of eggs before they run out of ideas.

Some decorations are suggested by the shape of the egg - Humpty Dumpty, a pig, a mouse, a fat cat - see what you can come up with together.

PUSSY CAT CANDLE HOLDERS

To make Salt Dough

1 In a large bowl, mix all ingredients well to make a firm dough. To keep pliable, cover with cling film or similar.

- 2 cups of plain flour
- 1 cup of salt
- 1 cup of water

Pussy Cat Holder

Materials:
- salt dough
- poster paints
- pencil
- paintbrush
- varnish
- small candle

Method:

1 Draw a rough sketch of the candle holder as a guide.

2 Taking a lump of dough, mould the body shape of a sitting cat. Mould on a piece of dough for a stumpy tail; a longer one can break when being 'cooked'. Make and attach two pointed ears.

TAIL

3 Using the end of a paintbrush, mark out the cat's features, lines for whiskers, fur and two front paws.

4 While the dough is still pliable, stick in the candle and make an indentation. Remove candle.

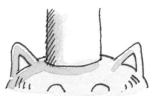

5 Stand on baking tray. 'Cook' in the oven for around four hours on a low heat (Gas mark $\frac{1}{2}$, 250°F/110°C).

6 Allow to cool completely. Paint. When dry, varnish and then set the candle in place.

Of course, your child might prefer to make an owl, or a bear, or a Santa Claus. Just follow the salt dough principle, but remember to keep the shape simple and 'dumpy'. Intricate pieces will fall off.

THE MOUSE FAMILY

Here's another salt dough suggestion. You'll find once children make one successful model, they won't want to stop!

When moulding the mice, they should be made different sizes.

Materials:
- salt dough
- poster paints
- paintbrush
- thin black ribbon
- varnish
- all-purpose glue

3 'Cook' in oven, as for Pussy Cat Candle Holder.

4 When completely cool, paint, either in natural colours or rainbow shades for fun. Cut lengths of ribbon and glue underneath for tails.

Method:

1 Taking a lump of dough, mould into mouse shapes, not forgetting little ears and a pointed nose.

2 With the blunt end of a paintbrush, mark in features and detail.

5 Finally, varnish.

HOOT THE BROWN OWL

Using materials you would otherwise throw away can produce inspiring work and creative results.

Materials:
- brown paper bag
- tissue paper
  (or other paper bags)
- cardboard
- scraps of felt
- felt-tipped pens
- glue
- scissors

Method:

1 Cut two feet shapes from card. Cut a triangular piece for the beak. Colour it in and fold it down the middle.

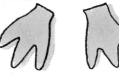

FOLD

2 Cut circles of felt for Hoot's eyes. These could be large white circles with smaller dark circles inside.

3 Draw two wings and cut them out. Colour them - with a feathery pattern if you like.

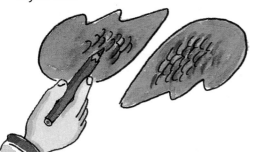

4 Cut a circle of card to fit the opening in the bag. Glue the feet to this.

UNDERNEATH

5 Stuff the bag with tissue or thin bags. Pull the top corners into 'ear' shapes. Snip round the bottom edge at about 1 cm intervals.

6 Glue these tabs and fold them around the edge of the base. Let it dry thoroughly and then glue on eyes, beak and wings.

You could make a simple perch for Hoot from a rolled piece of corrugated cardboard.

BUSY BUMBLE BEE MOBILE

Most children will love these bees, but the mobile can be decorated with many other flying creatures!

When you help to assemble it, remember a longer thread enables the bees to 'fly' in the breeze.

Materials:
- gold coloured card
- white paper
- black felt-tipped pen
- paper glue
- black thread
- two old metal coat hangers
- blue crepe paper
- scissors

Method:

1 Cut thin strips of crepe paper. Bind round the metal coat hangers. Glue the ends in place. Position the two covered hangers to form four sides, secure the hooks at the top of the thread making sure the hangers do not swing together.

SECURE WITH THREAD

2 On the gold card, fold the sheet over, and on one side draw the outline of a bumble bee, keeping the shape more oval than round. Cut round the shape carefully, so that you have two identical bees. Glue them together.

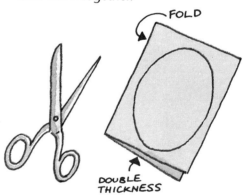

FOLD

DOUBLE THICKNESS

3 Mark on black stripes with the felt-tipped pen, and include eyes and a mouth.

4 For wings, cut out two small oval shapes in white paper. Glue onto the bee's body, one on either side.

5 Attach the bees to the coat hangers with long black threads. Put some on the corner, and some nearer the middle to make a well balanced mobile. Hang up high so that the bees move with the breeze.

Use red card with black spots for simple ladybird shapes. Butterflies are a simple outline with plenty of scope to let loose creative decoration ideas.

For brightly plumed birds use strips of coloured paper approximately 3 cm x 300 cm. Loop from one end to make a head, and finishing the figure-of-eight formation make a larger loop for the body. Glue the ends firmly to the centre of the loops. Add a beak, tail and legs. Pierce the top of the bird with the hanging thread and knot the end.

For slightly more unusual flying creatures, make pigs from circles of pink card. Snails can be made using strips of paper, as with the birds.

PAPER FANS

The fans look most attractive as wall decorations. Smaller versions can decorate a Christmas tree, if sprayed silver or gold.

Materials:
- good quality wrapping paper, patterned or plain - cut to size 33 x 48cm
- art paper, cartridge type - 33 x 48cm
- paper glue
- ribbon
- scissors
- ruler

Method:

1 Lay the wrapping paper out flat, brush on a layer of glue, making sure the entire surface is covered.

2 Stick it carefully and firmly onto the cartridge paper, smoothing it down well. Leave to dry for a few minutes.

3 Now mark and score lines on the back of the cartridge paper, approximately 3 cm wide.

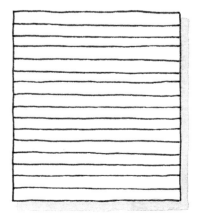

4 Holding the paper firmly, start folding along the lines. Whilst still holding the paper, cut a curve at the top.

CURVE

5 Secure the bottom of the fan with a piece of ribbon tied tightly, then open the fan out.

You could try many different designs as confidence increases. Use contrasting backing paper and ribbon.

Try a lace paper fan, glued onto a plain paper backing sheet.

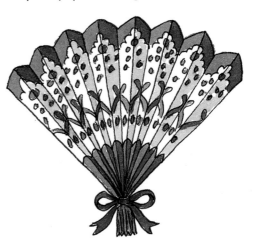

Glue a shallower piece of wrapping paper onto contrasting paper, both sheets patterned-side upwards, to make a 'two-tone' fan.

Use plain coloured, shaded paper with an edge of glitter dust.

Before gluing the sheets together, fold them as one. Separate the front sheet and cut diamonds and squares on the folds to create your own 'doily' effect. Now glue onto a plain backing sheet.

SILHOUETTE PICTURES

Creating silhouette pictures is challenging but, with a little practice, effective results can be achieved. This activity is only suitable for children who are able to use scissors safely.

Look around for original ideas. Children can try and make a 'rogues' gallery of the family, all cut out in silhouette. Here are just a couple of easier suggestions to start with.

Trace or draw an outline onto dark card, and mount it on a light background for maximum effect.

WOODLAND SILHOUETTE SCENE

Materials:
- large sheet of art card
- black sugar paper
- scissors
- paper glue
- pencil

Method:

1 Draw a series of trees lightly in pencil, and cut them out.
Some small, some larger, with twisting branches and gnarled trunks.

2 Now cut out a hedgehog and squirrel. Children can copy the outlines on this page.

3 Start building up your woodland scene. Position trees to look natural, glue in place. Place a squirrel on one of the branches, and the hedgehog somewhere in the foreground.
Glue in place.

More woodland creatures can be added as you like. Cut out some grasses or a fallen log to add interest.

BODY PARTS

Like Frankenstein, you can create monsters using all sorts of different body parts! Gruesome fun!

Materials:
- two identical boxes (lengthy biscuit boxes are ideal)
- knitting needle (or any long, thin axle)
- cotton reel
- card
- paper
- sticky tape
- glue

Method:

1 Cut the two equal-sided boxes in half.

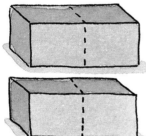

2 Glue the cotton reel in the middle of one box.

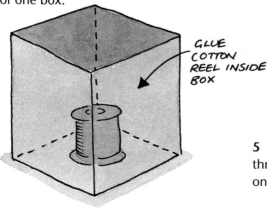

GLUE COTTON REEL INSIDE BOX

3 Cut four 'lids' from the card to fit over each box. Glue down.

4 Make a hole in the top and bottom of each box. The hole must be large enough for your axle to slide through. The hole must be in the centre of each square. Show your child how to find the centre of a square by drawing a line from corner to corner.

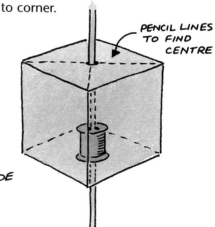

PENCIL LINES TO FIND CENTRE

5 Slot your needle (or whatever) through the cotton reel and then on through the holes.

6 Decide on four weird and wonderful characters, one for each side. Have fun creating monsters (and then *recreating* monsters once the boxes are able to revolve!).

Draw the head on the top box, followed by the body, then the legs and finally the feet on the bottom box.

By twisting each box, the child can create some very unusual characters! For example, their brother's head could be combined with the body of a orangutan, the legs of Popeye and the feet of a duck.

It might be easier to first draw your characters on paper, then glue them to the sides. For younger children, cut-outs from magazines might be easier still. Mix King Kong with a favourite cartoon character, and so on.

BIG FOOT SIZE CHART

The reverse of unwanted rolls of wallpaper or computer print-outs is ideal for larger works of art.

Materials:
- large sheet or roll of paper
- thick poster paint
- baking sheet or paint tray
- felt-tipped pens
- plenty of newspaper
- a willing family!

Method:

1 Spread the newspaper all over the floor. Secure your drawing paper in the middle with piles of magazines or papers.

2 Cover the bottom of the baking sheet or paint tray with paint. Each member of the family must take it in turns to dip one foot (wearing a wellington boot or old trainer, preferably) into the paint and make a careful print AT THE TOP OF THE PAPER. Each print must be upright and line up about 15 cm from the top.

3 Tidy away the mess from this stage whilst the paint dries.

4 Now turn the paper upside down and label each print - mum, dad, Tom, Jenny and so on. With felt-tips, add faces, limbs and a background to the frieze. Who has the biggest print? Are they also the tallest in the family?

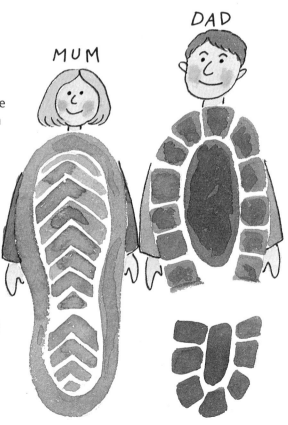

ANIMAL STONES

Children need to collect some fairly large, smooth, light coloured stones. When searching, they should look out for any whose shapes may suggest animals. The stones must be completely clean and dry before the fun can start.

Materials:
- stones
- acrylic paint
- paintbrushes
- clear varnish
- plenty of newspaper

When using acrylic paints, ensure that there is plenty of ventilation and don't leave children alone with paints.

Method:

1 Study the shape of a stone, and see what type of animal it might suggest. If no animal form is obvious, you may need to help your child by painting a simple animal outline onto the stone.

2 Use the paint thickly, to paint fur, limbs, a curled up tail, or spines. Be bold with the colours and accentuate the animal's features.

3 When dry, the animal stone can be finished with a coat of clear varnish.

Some likely animals may be mice, or a family of them, or a sleeping bear. Younger children may prefer a sea monster or a dinosaur.

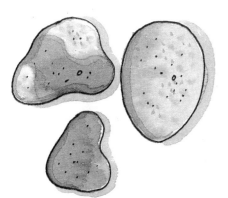

SPOOKY TREES

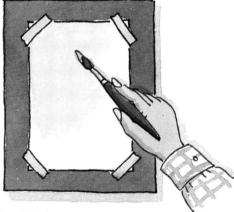

This is an ideal bit of fun for a rainy morning at home!

These fantastic trees emerge from poster paints. Children can choose to create the trees in any colour they like, but black or dark purple look most effective.

> **Materials:**
> - piece of board
> - art cartridge paper
> - poster paints
> - drinking straw
> - sticky tape
> - paintbrush
> - shallow bowl of water

Method:

1 Prepare the paper by dampening both sides with a little water. Secure the paper to a flat board with tape to stop it curling. Allow to dry.

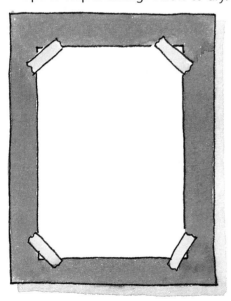

2 Moisten the paintbrush, and paint on a wash of pale blue, yellow or green paint. This background should cover all the paper.

3 Mix black or purple paint with water. With the clean paintbrush, drip on a few drops of paint along the bottom edge of the paper.

BLOBS OF RUNNY PAINT

4 Before this paint settles, take the straw and blow onto it to create the spooky trees. You will find that fantastic shapes appear. When dry, peel off the tape and trim the edges to neaten.

BLOW ON THE PAINT WITH THE STRAW

Really arty home-designed wrapping paper and gift tags can be made using the same method.

On a similar theme, you could create some amazing spooky spidery shapes with paint, paper, an orange, and a box lid.

Place your paper in the box lid. Pour two or three blobs of paint onto the paper. Now put a couple of oranges into the lid.

Roll the lid around so that the oranges zoom through the paint and around the paper. Don't let your child get over-exuberant, or you may end up with paint-covered oranges all over the floor!

SUPER STAINED GLASS

Keep a careful watch over this project - the principle is simple enough, but clingfilm can be dangerous near inquisitive faces.

Materials:
- microwave clingfilm
- poster paints
- thin paintbrush

Method:

1 Cut a piece of clingfilm of a manageable size. Fix it to a hard, flat surface, wrinkle-free.

STRETCH OUT SMOOTHLY

2 Load the brush with lots of paint. Your picture should not be too intricate, nor your painted lines too close.

3 Cut a second piece of clingfilm the same size as the first. Very carefully, lay it over the painting - you may need several pairs of helping hands!

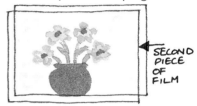

SECOND PIECE OF FILM

4 Spread and smooth the paint and the outsides of the clingfilm. The picture can be fixed to a window, making sure the paint does not dribble down. The thinner the paint is spread, the more transparent the colour becomes.

STAINED GLASS DIAMONDS

This design takes a little time to create, so won't suit the smaller child. It looks very good when complete, hung against the light.

> **Materials:**
> - sheet of art card
> - black sugar paper
> - selection of brightly coloured tissue paper
> - scissors
> - paper glue
> - ruler
> - pencil
> - string

Method:

1 Plan the design together before you start. Use the ruler to draw strips onto the sugar paper, then cut them out. These will be your diamond shapes.

2 Cut the card to form a frame, A4 size is sufficient.
(Younger children will need an adult's help here.)

3 Turn the card over, and begin gluing strips of the card, to form diamonds.

4 Still with the card reversed, cut and glue on pieces of coloured tissue paper, to fill the diamond windows. (Smaller children will love to do this, if you get them started.)

5 Turn the card over, attach a small piece of string and hang close to a window.

You can expand on this idea with your child. The same stained glass effect can be used for other silhouette pictures. A garden scene, or a bonfire night with fireworks against a dark sky are both good subjects.

CREATE-A-COLOUR

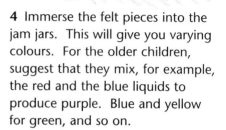

This messy project not only teaches children about colours, it also helps you dispose of all those leaky, old felt-tip pens that lurk in bedrooms!

Materials:
- old felt-tip pens
- plenty of newspapers
- jam jars
- scissors
- aprons/old t-shirts

Method:

1 Lay *plenty* of newspaper down. This is going to be VERY messy! Cover up all clothes.

2 Half fill the jam jars with water.

3 Break into the felt-tip pens to remove the length of felt inside. This can be quite tricky, so you might want to help the children with a kitchen knife. Use the knife, too, to open up the clear plastic surround.

4 Immerse the felt pieces into the jam jars. This will give you varying colours. For the older children, suggest that they mix, for example, the red and the blue liquids to produce purple. Blue and yellow for green, and so on.

FELT LINING

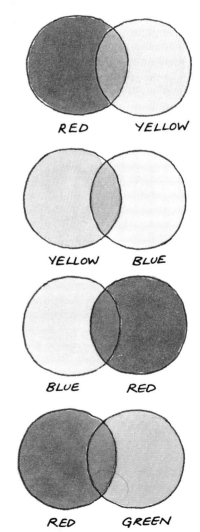

RED   YELLOW

YELLOW   BLUE

BLUE   RED

RED   GREEN

BUTTERFLY COLLAGE

A collage with a difference, this uses rose petals, gathered on a dry day. Tell a small child not to crush the petals - it will spoil the effect.

Press them between sheets of kitchen roll or blotting paper and leave for a few days under a heavy weight, like a phone book. Rose petals keep their colour this way and, some varieties, their perfume, too.

Materials:
- thick art paper
- quantity of prepared rose petals
- pencil and felt-tip pens
- all-purpose glue

Method:

1 Draw the outline of a butterfly, with wings open.

Draw in antennae in felt-tip pen.

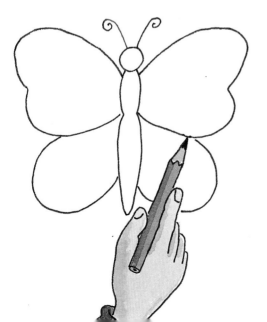

2 Your child should gently sort out the rose petals and, starting from one corner, glue them carefully onto the butterfly wings. They should overlap slightly, to avoid spaces showing.

3 Carry on until the wings are covered with petals.

4 Vary this idea with whole pressed pansy flowers or violets to make a lovely pattern for a homemade greetings card.

SEASIDE PLAQUE

When children are at the beach, get
them hunting for different shells,
pieces of driftwood, smooth polished
glass and other sea treasures washed
up by the tide. Often children have a
collection of these at home already,
so here's how they can be used.

Materials:
- large sheet of thick art card
- selection of shells, pebbles
  driftwood, polished glass, etc.
- paints
- paintbrush
- all-purpose glue
- scissors

Method:

1 Cut the card to a large oval shape.
Paint a border in bright blue to
suggest waves. Glue on a border
of small shells or intersperse with
tiny pebbles.

2 Paint on a wash of pale blue for
sky, and a darker blue for sea.
Add some creamy waves breaking on
the shore. Paint on gold and yellow
for the sand, and add some rocks to
one side of the beach. Allow to dry.

3 Now begin gluing on all the
seaside treasures. The trick is to
arrange the items to look natural.

COUNTRYSIDE COLLAGE

Collage stretches the imagination. Collect together all different kinds of paper, to introduce colours, textures and thicknesses. If you can look out of a window with your child, talk about the colours and the feel of the landscape, point out how the colours fade in the distance and seem brighter close up. Look closely at the shapes of trees, the way their branches reach to the sky.

This should be inspiration enough for a Four Seasons collage.

Materials:
- thick paper card
- different papers
- paper glue
- pencil
- felt-tip pens

Method:

1 Taking a pencil, draw some wavy lines across the paper, leaving different size gaps between the lines.

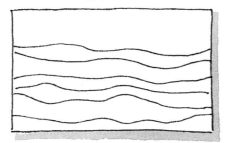

2 Carefully choose about seven different kinds of paper. They could be from a magazine, newspaper, wallpaper, wrapping paper.

3 Now start building up your collage. Tear off little pieces of paper, stick in the gaps between the lines. You don't have to be too precise, but try to fill most of the spaces.

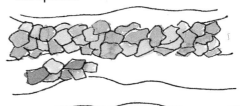

4 Using felt-tips, draw in some trees, and a few more details, maybe some birds flying overhead, or a small farmhouse in the distance. You could also colour in some sky and clouds.

SAM SCARECROW

This is a jolly activity but its success hinges on having the right fabric glue. Younger children can get really involved with this, but will need supervision when it comes to drawing outlines and cutting out.

Materials:
- sheet of thick card
  (or empty cereal carton)
- material scraps
- glue (such as latex glue)
- felt-tip pens
- string
- wool

Method:

1 Draw a Sam Scarecrow outline on a large sheet of card, complete with top hat. With felt pens, colour in his features.

2 Starting with his coat, cut out material to shape his body. Glue in place.

3 Next the trousers, using contrasting cloth for the patches.

4 Cut a piece of string and glue around his waist. Fray a small piece and glue on for his hands.

5 For his hair, cut short strands of wool and glue down. Cover the top hat in fabric to fit the shape you have drawn. Cut a flower shape from cloth and glue to the hat.

Don't expect the result to be too neat, especially if younger children are really participating.
Sam Scarecrow can look very effective in a loose, scarecrow-like way!

6 Children can finish the collage as they wish, using felt-tips freehand, to draw a cornfield or fields behind.

LOLLY CARD

Collage is a lovely technique to show off on cards for all occasions. Make them a little bit more special still by adding a sweet treat to the front!

Materials:
- stiff card, 24 cm x 15 cm
- collage materials as per previous page
- lollipop

1 Fold the card in half.

2 Draw your outline on what will be the front of the greetings card. Use Sam Scarecrow to start with if you like.

3 By Sam's hand, pierce two small slits for the lollipop stick to slot through.

4 Fill Sam in with material and string, keeping the hand slits clear.

5 Slot the lolly in place and write your message on the inside.

PAPIER MÂCHÉ MASKS

This is an ideal home activity, to while away hours very productively. It can be a very sticky business so children should be well covered up, and surrounded by plenty of old newspaper.

The same method is used to make all three masks described.

Materials:
- medium-sized pudding basin
- Vaseline jelly
- wallpaper paste
- paintbrush (small - 2.5 cm)
- small plastic bowl
  (for mixing paste in)
- old newspaper

For the masks:
- paint
- all-purpose glue
- coloured card
- sharp scissors
- glitter dust
- thin elastic or string

Method:

1 Tear pieces of newspaper into strips.

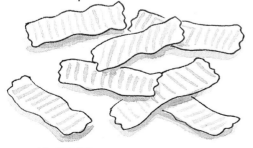

2 Spread a thin layer of Vaseline over half the pudding basin (on the outside).

3 Mix up some wallpaper paste into plastic bowl. Dip torn newspaper strips into the paste.

4 Place on your basin so that the strips overlap. Be sure to cover up all the part covered by Vaseline.

5 Brush paste over the strips, using the paintbrush. Then start another layer of paper strips.

6 Carry on this way until you have built up about five or six layers. If children have the patience, it is best to allow the two first layers to dry before adding any more.

7 When the bowl is completely dry, the papier mâché feels hard to the touch. Take it off the mould carefully. Neaten the edges.

TRIM EDGES

CLEVER CAT

1 Cut slanted eyes in the mask, for cat's eyes.

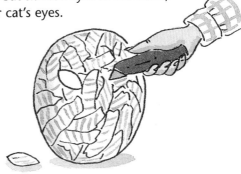

2 Paint in stripes in black or colour preferred. Accentuate the eyes and paint on a pink nose.

3 Cut thin strips of card for whiskers. Stick onto mask.

4 Attach the mask with thin elastic, or pieces of ribbon to hold it on your child's head.

5 For a very special party cat, put on dabs of glue and then sprinkle on coloured glitter.

RAINBOW MASKS

1 Cut two slits for eyes.

2 Carefully paint the colours of the rainbow in curves, starting from the bottom of the mask.

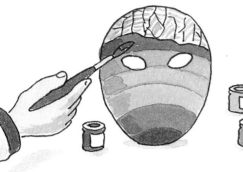

3 Stroke on some glue to follow the curve of the design and sprinkle on gold or silver glitter.

4 Attach the mask with elastic or ribbon.

FUNNY FACE

1 Cut around holes for eyes and a mouth.

2 Paint the mask in crazy colours - children can go wild with the colours. Outline the eyes with long black lashes, and paint a red mouth.

3 Cut out some card and make wild hair. Glue onto inside of mask.

4 Attach the mask with elastic or ribbon.

Once children have successfully made a simple mask, they will be keen to make more original designs and add papier mâché ears, horns or noses, moulded over a variety of household objects. Experimenting can be enormous fun.

PAPIER MÂCHÉ BOWL

Papier mâché is versatile and surprisingly durable. To make a decorative bowl, which might make a good present for a teacher or grandparent, use the same method as for the masks on the previous pages. This time, however, use a small bowl as the form to cover.

When the papier mâché is completely dry, it can be decorated simply or elaborately.

1 Paint the inside one colour, and the outside a contrasting colour.

Pick out lines or swirls with a thin paintbrush for detail.

2 A thin coat of clear varnish applied to the bone-dry bowl will give it a lasting glossy finish and heighten the colour of the paints used. This also protects it from moisture marks but is not essential.

YOU COULD FILL A BOWL WITH SOME HOME MADE POT POURRI (P. 47)

TAMBOURINE

Whilst you're up to your elbows in papier mâché, you could direct the making of this simple 'musical' instrument (no promises about the 'tunes' that will come forth, though).

Materials:
- papier mâché strips
- thick card
- bottle tops, washers, ring-pulls
- cocktail sticks
- masking tape (or sticky tape)
- paints

Method:

1 Cut the card into a strip about 5 cm x 50 cm. Curl into a band and secure the ends with masking tape. (Sticky tape may be used, but won't cover so well with the papier mâché.)

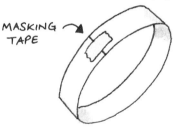

MASKING TAPE

2 Cut four or five wide slits around the band. Thread the 'jangly' bits onto cocktail sticks and secure to the band, so they move and jangle within the slits.

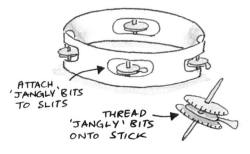

ATTACH 'JANGLY' BITS TO SLITS

THREAD 'JANGLY' BITS ONTO STICK

3 Cover the whole band with layers of papier mâché and leave to dry thoroughly.

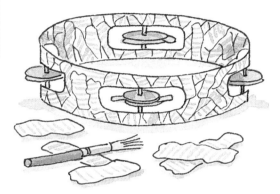

4 Decorate the instrument in bright colours and patterns.

EASY TO MAKE POT POURRI

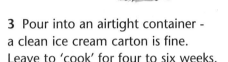

Children will be repeating the steps of children down the centuries, making this simple recipe. This activity will encourage observation and value for natural things. And the result is an ozone-friendly perfume for any room in the house.

Materials:
- 2 cups of dried rose petals
- 2 cups of dried lavender flowers
- 1 cup of dried lemon mint leaves (or similar)
- ½ cup of coarse salt
- 1 tablespoon of mixed spice (powder)
- small quantity of pink statice flowers to scatter on top

Method:

1 It is important the flowers are completely dry before you start, as any damp ones will turn the pot pourri mouldy.

2 Put all the ingredients in a large glass mixing bowl. Mix gently to make sure the salt and spices are blended well.

3 Pour into an airtight container - a clean ice cream carton is fine. Leave to 'cook' for four to six weeks.

4 Display in pretty dishes around the home.

Nearly all scented flowers, leaves and herbs are suitable for pot pourri. Adding salt and spices acts as a fixing agent or preservative to keep the delicate fragrance. Orris root and dried citrus fruit skins are also effective.

Children can then experiment with their own mixtures, adding wood bark or nut kernels, acorn cups, bay leaves and other finds from a country walk.

MOUSEY MARKERS

These handy clip-ons can be used around the house, but are ideal for keeping place in the pages of a book.

Materials:
- scraps of felt
- old-fashioned curl clips (with springs)
- fabric glue
- scissors

1 Draw a simple mouse template - an egg with a pointed nose! Cut four of these from felt.

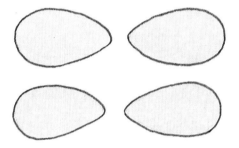

2 Glue the shapes around the 'arms' of the clip. Glue two together over one arm, two over the other. Leave the end of the clip uncovered, to lever the two parts open.

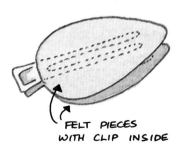

FELT PIECES WITH CLIP INSIDE

3 Cut ears, eyes and a little round nose-tip to glue on to the top. Whiskers could be made from lengths of cotton sewn through the nose, and a tail from string or felt.

4 Leave mousey to dry thoroughly before using him to mark your page.

Home STICKY FINGERS